A TRUE BOOK™

SURVIVAL SKILLS
WATER
FIRE
FOOD

Diane Vukovic

Children's Press®
An imprint of Scholastic Inc.

SAFETY NOTE

This book suggests several survival skills techniques. When possible, they should all be done with adult supervision. Observe safety and caution at all times. The author and publisher disclaim all liability for any damage, mishap, injury, illness, or death that may occur from engaging in the survival skills techniques featured in this book or any other use of this book.

Special thanks to our content consultant, Ben McNutt, who has been teaching wilderness bushcraft and survival skills while leading remote expeditions to forest, jungle, desert, and frozen environments for more than 20 years. Ben also runs courses at wildhuman.com.

Library of Congress Cataloging-in-Publication Data
Names: Vukovic, Diane, author. | Francis, Kate, 1976– illustrator.
Title: Water, fire, food / Diane Vukovic; illustrations by Kate Francis.
Description: First edition. | New York, NY: Children's Press, an imprint of Scholastic Inc., 2023. | Series: A true book: Survival skills | Includes bibliographical references and index. | Audience: Ages 8–10 | Audience: Grades 4–6 | Summary: "A new installment in the A True Book series focusing on Survival Skills"—Provided by publisher.
Identifiers: LCCN 2022022895 (print) | LCCN 2022022896 (ebook) | ISBN 9781338853629 (library binding) | ISBN 9781338853636 (paperback) | ISBN 9781338853643 (ebk)
Subjects: LCSH: Wilderness survival—Juvenile literature. | Survival—Juvenile literature. | BISAC: JUVENILE NONFICTION / Sports & Recreation / Camping & Outdoor Activities | JUVENILE NONFICTION / General
Classification: LCC GV200.5 .V859 2023 (print) | LCC GV200.5 (ebook) | DDC 613.6/9—dc23/ eng/20220613
LC record available at https://lccn.loc.gov/2022022895
LC ebook record available at https://lccn.loc.gov/2022022896

10 9 8 7 6 5 4 3 2 1   23 24 25 26 27

Printed in China, 62
First edition, 2023

Design by Kathleen Petelinsek
Series produced by Spooky Cheetah Press

Find the Truth!

Everything you are about to read is true *except* for one of the sentences on this page.

Which one is **TRUE**?

T or F   Most insects are edible.

T or F   Rubbing two sticks together is a good way to start a fire.

Find the answers in this book.

What's in This Book?

Most water needs
to be treated
before drinking.

4

Plants can provide water as well as food.

Avoid eating mushrooms. They can be deadly!

Skills for a Lifetime

For most of the time that humans have been on Earth, there were no supermarkets, running water, or electric stoves and heaters. Yet early humans were **able to survive and thrive**, even in very tough climates. They did this by **using survival skills**.

A survivalist is someone who practices outdoor survival skills.

If you were ever **lost in the wilderness**, you would use many of the same **skills to survive**. Luckily, most of us will never find ourselves in a true survival situation. However, these skills are still important to learn. Knowing how to **find water and food** and being able to **make fire** will make you feel **more confident in the wilderness**. It will also help you appreciate the great outdoors!

Only about 1.2 percent of the water on Earth is safe to drink.

Always carry plenty of drinking water when you go out adventuring!

Water in the Wilderness

Humans can survive for about three days without water. But if you don't drink water, you can begin to feel symptoms of **dehydration**—exhaustion, dizziness, and confusion—sooner than that. If it is very hot outside, dehydration can occur in just a few hours. That is why finding water is considered a survival priority. That can be difficult in some places. And even if you can find water, it might not be safe to drink. Luckily, there are lots of ways to make water safe to drink.

Some bacteria are hundreds of times smaller than the width of a human hair!

Standing water, like ponds and lakes, can be particularly unsafe.

What's in Water?

Water from streams, rivers, lakes, and other natural sources may *look* clean. But it can contain **pathogens** like bacteria, parasites, algae, and viruses that can make you sick. You will dehydrate faster if you are puking or rushing to the bathroom every 10 minutes! That is why it is important that you treat water before drinking it. Treating water means removing harmful substances like pathogens so the water is safe to drink.

Ways to Treat Water

Hikers and backpackers often carry special filters to treat water. The filters have very tiny holes that allow water to pass through but keep bacteria, algae, and parasites out. If you don't have a filter, you can treat water by heating it to a rapid boil for three minutes. That will kill or deactivate any pathogens. If the water is really dirty, you can filter it through a bandanna or T-shirt before boiling. The cloth filter alone won't remove pathogens, though, so it's important to still boil the water.

Hikers may also carry water treatment tablets. Those kill or deactivate most pathogens.

If You Can't Treat Water

What if there is water nearby but you don't have a way to treat it? If the choice is between dehydration and drinking untreated water, then it's better to drink the water. Just remember that some sources of water are safer than others. Bacteria and algae grow very easily in still water, so you should avoid drinking water from ponds and lakes if possible. Instead, try to choose water from a moving source, like a stream or spring. There still may be harmful pathogens in the water, but there will probably be fewer of them, so you might not get sick.

Collecting Rainwater

When water **evaporates** into the air, harmful pathogens are left behind. That's why, in a survival situation, rainwater doesn't need to be treated before drinking. However, you can't just leave a water bottle outside in the rain and expect it to fill up—that would take too long! Instead, you should make a rainwater collector. Hang a tarp or plastic sheet so one part is angled toward your water container. The tarp has a larger surface area than the mouth of your water bottle. It collects more water quickly and then funnels it into your container.

A tarp is an essential survival tool.

It could take more than **300 hours** to fill a standard water bottle during a light rain shower. With a small tarp it could take less than **30 minutes**!

Distilling Safe Water

A solar still is another way to get safe drinking water. It works by solar distillation. That is a process that uses the sun's energy to separate impurities from water. It has to be hot outside for a solar still to work. Heat will cause water inside the still to evaporate— leaving behind salt, pathogens, dirt, and other substances you don't want to drink. The evaporated water hits the top of the still, where it **condenses** and drips down into your collection container.

HOW TO MAKE A SOLAR STILL

1 Dig a hole about 2 feet (0.6 meters) around and 6 inches (15 centimeters) deep.

2 Place leaves, grass, or other wet items in the hole. You can also place a container of salt water or dirty water inside.

3 Place a container for collecting clean water in the center of the hole.

4 Completely cover the hole with a piece of plastic. Use rocks to hold the plastic in place.

5 Add a small rock in the middle of the plastic. It should be heavy enough to make the plastic dip down.

6 Wait. It can take all day to collect just a small sip of water!

A solar still is the only do-it-yourself way to make salt water safe to drink.

Water from Trees

Did you know that plants "breathe"? As they take in carbon dioxide from the air, they release oxygen and clean water, which you can trap and pour into a container to drink. (Or drink it right from the bag!)

HOW TO CAPTURE WATER FROM TREES

1 Find a tree or bush with lots of green leaves. (Avoid the manchineel tree—it is highly toxic.)

The manchineel tree is found on sandy beaches in the Caribbean and along the Gulf of Mexico.

WARNIN

2 Place a clear plastic bag around the leaves. Try to get as many leaves in there as you can!

3 Tie the bag closed.

4 Wait. After several hours, you should see water starting to collect in the bag. You can pour it into your mouth.

It takes all day to get a bit of water this way, but every little bit helps!

4

Make sure to close up the bag secure

Collecting Dew

Even though we can't see it, there is usually a lot of water in the air. The water is invisible because

Green leafy plants are a good source of dew.

it is in a gas form called **water vapor**. Cold air can't hold as much vapor as warm air can. That is why at night, as the temperature drops, water vapor condenses. It turns into the small droplets of water we call dew. In the early morning, when there is the most dew, press a cloth (like a bandanna) onto the wet grass or leaves. Then wring out the cloth into your water bottle. Some dirt or pathogens might get mixed in with the dew water. If possible, filter the dew before drinking it. But in a true survival situation, you can even wring the dew water directly into your mouth.

Water from Snow

If you are lost in winter, you may be tempted to eat snow for water. Don't do it! It takes energy for your body to turn the snow into water. That can lower your body temperature dangerously. You need to melt snow before drinking it. There are three easy ways to do that.

1 **Melting snow using fire:** Gather snow in a pot and place it on a camp stove or next to a fire. You'll need to add a bit of water to the bottom of the pot as a "starter." Otherwise, you'll scorch the pot before the snow can melt.

As the snow melts, add more to the pot.

2 **Melting snow using indirect heat:** You can also gather snow in a cloth bag or an extra shirt. Hang the bag from a tree branch or a tripod made from sticks. Place your water container under the bag. Make a fire about 2 feet (0.6 m) from the bag. As heat from the fire melts the snow, water will drip into your container.

③ **Melting snow using the sun:** If you can't make a fire, you can still melt snow if the sun is shining. Place something dark, like a black trash bag, in a sunny spot. Fill your water bottle with snow and place it on top of the bag. Heat from the sun will melt the snow.

Gather snow from deep drifts so you don't end up with dirt in your water.

Snow is mostly made up of air. It takes a lot of snow to get a bit of water.

Don't put an insulated or double-wall metal bottle on a fire. It could explode!

⚠ WARNING

A campfire is also helpful in that it will lift your spirits—even if you are lost.

Fire needs oxygen to burn. That is why Earth is the only known planet where fires can burn.

Making Fire

Our ancestors started using fire more than one million years ago, and it's one of the key things that helped them survive. Even today, firecraft—knowing how to make and control a fire—is an incredibly important skill. A fire keeps you warm. It can also be used to signal for help, purify water, boil water to **sterilize** bandages and utensils, cook food, and keep animals (including pesky mosquitoes!) away. Making a fire is also a skill that you can use on outdoor adventures where it is allowed.

Before Lighting a Fire

Nearly 85 percent of wildfires in the United States are caused by people. That's why it's so important to follow a few simple rules. Sparks can fly far, so make sure to build your fire at least 10 feet (3 m) away from anything that can catch fire, like trees, bushes, and your shelter. Clear any dry brush from your fire-making area. Then make a fire ring by digging a pit or placing large rocks in a circle. These help contain the fire so it doesn't spread.

Timeline: Fire-Making Techniques

AT LEAST 1 MILLION YEARS AGO
Early humans save hot ash or burning wood from forest or grass fires to make fire for warmth and cooking.

AT LEAST 50,000 YEARS AGO
Humans bang together rocks containing flint and pyrite to start fires.

AT LEAST 7,000 YEARS AGO
Bow drills and fire saws are used to start a fire with **friction**.

Tinder, Kindling, and Fuel

Tinder, kindling, and fuel wood are the "ingredients" needed to make a fire. You'll need to collect lots of each before getting started. Tinder is made up of very small dry materials that will light easily. Tiny sticks, paper, and cotton balls coated in petroleum jelly all make good tinder. The tinder is used to light kindling—small sticks about as thick as your finger. The kindling then ignites the fuel wood, made up of thicker branches and logs. Fuel wood releases lots of heat and burns for a long time.

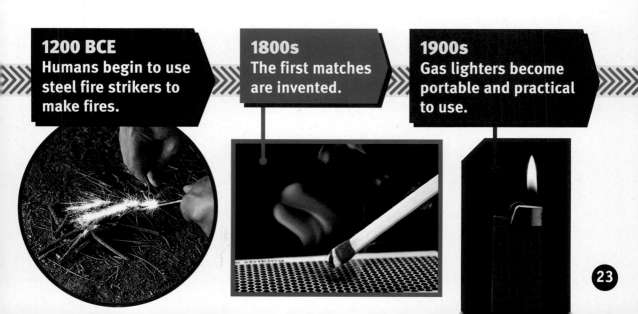

1200 BCE
Humans begin to use steel fire strikers to make fires.

1800s
The first matches are invented.

1900s
Gas lighters become portable and practical to use.

Building the Fire

The tepee shape helps more oxygen get to the fire.

To get a fire going, you need to position the tinder, kindling, and fuel wood so each one lights the other. The simplest way to do this is with the tepee fire lay.

HOW TO MAKE A TEPEE FIRE LAY

1 Place a pile of tinder in the center of your fire ring or pit.

2 Starting with your smallest kindling, make a tepee over the tinder. Leave a little "door" in the tepee so you can still reach the tinder.

3 Add more kindling to make the tepee bigger.

4 Place several pieces of fuel wood over the tepee. You'll add more later as the fire burns down.

5 Reach through the door to light the tinder.

Signaling for Help

Making a fire is one of the best ways to signal for help at night. "Three" is the universal signal for **distress**, so you will need to make *three* fires—not just one. Place the fires in a triangle shape. Otherwise, they might just look like one big

Smoke signals can help rescuers find you if you're lost.

fire to a plane passing overhead. It's hard to see a fire during the daytime, so you'll want to make smoke signals during the day instead. To do this, gather lots of green vegetation like leaves and moss. Then pile the vegetation on top of the fires to create smoke.

You can also signal for help by blowing a whistle or banging on something three times. Repeat.

Making a Fire in the Rain

You may be surprised to learn that you can even make a fire in the rain! To do so, use the Lean-to fire lay, which uses layers of wood. The top layer acts like a roof to protect the lower layers from the rain. As the lower layers burn, they dry out the top layers of wood.

HOW TO MAKE A LEAN-TO FIRE LAY

1 Lay sticks flat on the ground to make a platform for your fire. Otherwise, the wet ground will extinguish your fire.

2 Find a large log and place it next to your platform.

Never make a fire inside your shelter— even in a cave.

3 Find dry tinder and some dry kindling. The sticks underneath piles of debris are often dry. Gather additional kindling, which doesn't have to be dry, and fuel wood.

4 Place a pile of dry tinder on the platform. Place the dry kindling over the tinder so it is leaning on the log.

5 Add more layers of kindling. This kindling doesn't need to be very dry. Top with small fuel wood logs, which work better than large fuel wood in the rain.

6 Light the tinder. There will be a lot of smoke at first as the kindling dries out, but a fire should get going.

7 As the fire burns, keep adding more fuel wood to the "roof" so rain can't get to the fire below.

How to Start a Fire Without Matches

It is important that you always bring a fire-starting kit with you on outdoor adventures. The kit should include dry tinder, matches that have been stored in a waterproof container, and a backup fire starter (such as a lighter). If you forget your kit, however, you might be able to get a fire going using one of these three methods. They will take more effort, but they can work!

Battery Trick

Cut a gum wrapper into a thin strip. Ask an adult to touch it to both ends of a battery at the same time. Electric current from the battery will flow through the wrapper and cause it to catch fire. Quickly use the flame to light tinder.

Knife and Rock

Steel contains iron, which is one of the most flammable materials in the world. If an adult bangs a hard rock like flint or quartz on the back of a closed steel pocketknife, the impact will cause tiny pieces of iron to fly out as sparks. Quickly use the sparks to light tinder.

Lens

Magnifying glasses have convex lenses on both sides. That means the lenses curve outward in both directions. This shape bends and focuses light into a powerful beam. On a sunny day, use a magnifying glass to aim the hot light beam toward tinder to ignite it.

Many people around the world forage for their food.

Try to learn about edible plants in your area before heading out on a hike.

CHAPTER 3

Finding Food

Humans can survive for three weeks without food, so it is not one of the top survival priorities when you are lost. In fact, it's better to be hungry than to eat something that could make you sick or even kill you! There is no reason you should ever go hungry in the wilderness, though. Searching for food in the wild is called **foraging**. And all you need for foraging is a bit of knowledge.

Edible Plants

There are about 400,000 **species** of plants in the world, and at least 20,000 of these are edible. So there are probably lots of edible plants where you live—maybe even in your backyard. Here are some of the most common and easily recognizable edible plants in North America.

Dandelions: Though it's not the tastiest of plants (it's very bitter!), you can eat all parts of the dandelion except the stem. Unless your life depends on it, though, don't munch on dandelions that might have been sprayed by weed killer or other chemicals.

Dandelions

Dandelions contain lots of iron, calcium, and vitamin C.

Cattail plants: You can often find cattails growing near ponds and lakes. The roots, stalks, and shoots are all edible. You can also eat the tops of cattails before they turn to fluff.

Cattails

Cleavers: This plant is easy to identify by its pointy narrow leaves that circle the stalk and are sticky to the touch. The leaves are edible and taste a bit like young peas. The seeds contain caffeine.

Cleavers

Plantago: This is a very hardy weed that grows almost everywhere in the world. The leaves are a bit bitter and stringy, but the young seed shoots have a nice nutty taste.

Plantago

Wild blueberries

POISONOUS ! WARNING

Tutsan berries

Wild carrot

POISONOUS ! WARNING

Hemlock

Never eat a plant if you are not 100 percent sure of what it is!

Poisonous Look-Alikes

A lot of common edible plants have poisonous look-alikes. For example, tutsan berries are **toxic**. But they are easy to mistake for wild blueberries, which are edible. Wild carrot, which is one of the most common edible plants in North America, looks very similar to hemlock, which is poisonous. Foragers learn about the small differences in these plants so they can correctly identify them.

Don't Mess with Mushrooms

Mushroom hunters will often say, "You can eat any mushroom . . . once." That means some mushrooms are so deadly that eating them will kill you. There are no second chances! The problem is that some edible and poisonous mushrooms look remarkably similar. Often the only way to tell them apart is by tiny details. So unless you are an experienced mushroom hunter, you should never eat any wild mushrooms.

Symptoms from toxic mushrooms can appear anywhere from 30 minutes to six hours after eating.

This mushroom, called death cap, accounts for 90 percent of all deaths from mushrooms.

⚠ WARNING

Remove legs and wings before eating insects. They'll go down easier!

Cricket flour contains twice as much protein as beef!

Eating Insects

There is actually a great source of food that is readily available in the wilderness: insects. Almost all insects are edible, including most beetles and their **larvae**, as well as ants, crickets, and grasshoppers. Many insects are highly nutritious, too. Best of all, they are easy to find. Just lift up a dead log or rock and you'll probably find some grubs to eat. In a survival situation, you can eat raw insects. But, just like with meat, it's safer to cook them first.

Building an Insect Trap

A pitfall trap is used to catch insects that crawl on the ground. To make one, first find a container with an open top, such as a yogurt cup or plastic bottle with the top cut off. Then dig a hole in the ground.

Place the container in the hole so the top is level with the ground. Fill any gaps between the hole and the container with dirt. Place four rocks or sticks around the edge of the trap to make "legs." Prop something flat, like a piece of plastic, on top of the legs. Check the trap every 12 to 24 hours.

The covering on the trap is to protect it from rain.

Lots of people around the world regularly eat locusts, which are a type of grasshopper.

Cooking Over a Fire

Now that you've caught some food, it's time to cook it. If you don't have a pan or grill rack and the food is too small to roast on a stick, you can use a "frying rock."

HOW TO MAKE A FRYING ROCK

⚠️ **WARNING** It is important to choose the right rock. Igneous rocks and porous rocks like sandstone (above) are fine. But flint, chert, obsidian, concrete, or river rocks (below) should not be used. They will explode when heated.

1 Find a large, flat rock. Don't use rocks you find in or near water. They might have water inside them and could explode if heated! If you aren't sure, place the rock into the fire and walk 100 feet (30 m) away. If the fire dies down and the rock is still in one piece, it's safe to use for cooking.

2 Prop the frying rock up on some smaller rocks so it's about 1 foot (0.3 m) off the ground.

3 Make a small fire underneath the frying rock. Keep feeding the fire with kindling. The flames should barely touch the bottom of the rock.

4 Place food on top of the rock to cook.

You don't have to wait for a survival situation to try this or other skills like collecting water or making a fire. Practicing survival skills doesn't just ensure that you will be prepared if something unexpected happens—it can be a lot of fun, too!

SISTERS SURVIVE
Two Nights Lost in Wilderness

Leia (left) and Caroline (right) were happy to have each other for company!

Sisters Leia (8) and Caroline (5) Carrico were allowed to play in the woods near their California home, but their dad told them never to go past a certain tree. One day the girls wanted "more adventure," so they decided to hike a bit farther than allowed. They walked for a while, and after hiking past the same spot, the girls realized they had gone in a giant circle and didn't know how to get home. It was close to freezing outside and getting dark. It had also started to rain. Luckily, the girls had learned some survival skills from a local youth club and on camping trips. They knew to stay put and wait for help. To stay dry and warm, they found a natural shelter beneath a bush and huddled together under Caroline's rain jacket. The girls also knew rainwater was safe to drink, so they drank raindrops off some huckleberry leaves. Local search teams found Leia and Caroline 44 hours after they were reported lost. The girls were hungry, cold, and a bit dehydrated, but otherwise safe and in good spirits.

Rescuers had food ready for the girls when they found them.

Use what you learned in this book to answer the questions below.

1 Which of these three things do you need to take care of first if you are lost in the woods?

    A. Fire   **C**. Water

    B. Food

2 How long should you boil water to make it safe to drink?

3 Which of the following do typical camping filters remove from water?

    A. Bacteria   **D**. Viruses

    B. Parasites   **E**. Chemicals

    C. Algae

4 TRUE or FALSE: You should eat snow if you are thirsty.

5 What method could you use to make saltwater drinkable?

A

B

C

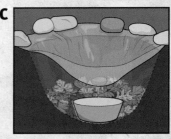

6 Name each type of fire-making material shown below.

A

B

C

7 Which picture shows a lean-to fire lay?

A

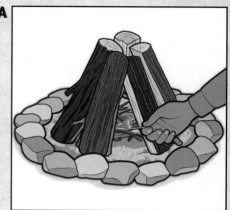

B

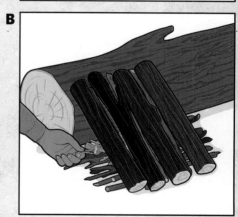

8 What is the universal signal for distress?

Number of people who get sick from waterborne disease in the United States every year: More than 7 million

How long a person can live without water: About 3 days

How long a person can live without food: About 3 weeks

Amount of water released into the air by a large oak tree: About 100 gallons (379 liters) per day

Percentage of wildfires caused by humans: Nearly 85%

Temperature of a typical campfire: Around 900°F (482°C)

Number of wild edible plants in North America: At least 4,000

Percentage of wild mushrooms that are poisonous to humans: 1%–2%

Did you find the truth?

T Most insects are edible.

F Rubbing two sticks together is a good way to start a fire.

Resources

Other books in this series:

You can also look at:

Colson, Rob. *Ultimate Survival Guide for Kids*. Ontario, Canada: Firefly Books, 2015.

Grindrod, Frank. *Wilderness Adventure Camp: Essential Outdoor Survival Skills for Kids*. North Adams, MA: Storey, 2021.

Sumerak, Marc. *Survival Handbook: An Essential Companion to the Great Outdoors*. Bellevue, WA: becker&mayer! kids, 2019.

Glossary

condenses (kuhn-DEN-siz) changes from a gas into a liquid, usually as a result of cooling

dehydration (dee-hye-DRAY-shuhn) abnormal depletion of body fluids, which are necessary for proper function

distress (di-STRES) in need of help

evaporates (i-VAP-uh-rates) changes from a liquid into a vapor or gas

foraging (FOR-ij-ing) going in search of food

friction (FRIK-shuhn) the rubbing of one object against another

larvae (LAHR-vee) insects at the stage of development between an egg and a pupa, when they look like worms

pathogens (PATH-uh-jenz) agents that cause disease, such as bacteria and viruses

species (SPEE-sheez) one of the groups into which animals and plants of the same genus are divided

sterilize (STER-uh-lize) to rid someting of germs and dirt by filtering it, heating it, and/or treating it

toxic (TAHK-sik) poisonous

water vapor (WAW-tur VAY-pur) water in the form of a gas

Index

Page numbers in **bold** indicate illustrations.

About the Author

Diane Vukovic is an expert camper, backpacker, and disaster-preparedness specialist. It all started when she was a kid living in upstate New York and would spend her free time exploring the woods near her home, making forts and going on backpacking trips with her dad and sister. Now Diane has two daughters of her own and loves taking them on wilderness camping trips and teaching them survival skills like first aid and shelter-making. She also loves to travel to remote, lesser-known parts of the world and has been to more than 30 countries on six continents. Diane shares her knowledge at momgoescamping.com and primalsurvivor.net.